# THAILAND

# MAJOR WORLD NATIONS
# THAILAND

Frances Wilkins

## CHELSEA HOUSE PUBLISHERS
Philadelphia

**Chelsea House Publishers**

Copyright © 2000 by Chelsea House Publishers,
a division of Main Line Book Co.
All rights reserved.
Printed in Malaysia

First Printing.

1 3 5 7 9 8 6 4 2

Library of Congress Cataloging-in-Publication Data

Wilkins, Frances.
[Let's visit Thailand]
Thailand / Frances Wilkins.
p.    cm. — (Major world nations)
Includes index.
Summary: Describes the geography, history, people, and customs of Thailand.
ISBN 0-7910-5400-4 (hc)
1. Thailand—Juvenile literature. [1. Thailand.] I. Title.
II. Series.
DS563.5.W55    1999
959.3—dc21       99-11833
CIP

ACKNOWLEDGEMENTS

The Author and Publishers are grateful to the following organizations and individuals
for permission to reproduce copyright photographs in this book:
Colorpix, Imag, International Photobank, Eugénie Peter and
PhotothéqueVautier-de Nanxe

# CONTENTS

MYANMAR
(BURMA)

LAOS

Chiang
Rai

Chiang
Mai

Lamphun

Mekong River

Sukhothai

Khon
Kaen

Chao Phraya River

River Kwai

Ubon

Lop Buri

Surin

Kanchana-
buri

Ayutthaya

Nakhon
Pathom

Bangkok

ANDAMAN
SEA

Damnoen
Saduak

Pattaya

CAMBODIA

VIETNAM

Phuket

GULF OF THAILAND

THAILAND

Songkhla

0    100    200    300 Kms

Hat
Yai

0         100         200

MALAYSIA

N

# FACTS AT A GLANCE

## Land and People

**Official Name** Kingdom of Thailand

**Location** Center of mainland Southeast Asia

**Area** 198,115 square miles (513,115 square kilometers)

**Climate** Tropical; rainy and warm mid-May to September, dry and cool November to mid-March

**Capital** Bangkok

**Other Cities** Chiang Mai, Ayutthaya, Nakhon Ratchasima

**Population** 60,037,366

**Major Rivers** Chao Phraya, Mekong, Pa Sak

**Highest Point** Doi Inthanon, 2,576 meters

**Official Language** Thai

**Other Languages** English, ethnic and regional dialects

**Ethnic Groups** Thai, 75 percent; Chinese, 14 percent

**Religions** Buddhism, 95 percent

**Literacy Rate** 93.8 percent

| | |
|---|---|
| **Average Life Expectancy** | 69 years |

# Economy

| | |
|---|---|
| **Natural Resources** | Tin, rubber, natural gas, tungsten, timber, fish, lead |
| **Division of Labor Force** | Agriculture, 54 percent; industry, 15 percent; services, 31 percent |
| **Agricultural Products** | Rice, cassava, rubber, corn, sugarcane, coconuts, soybeans |
| **Industries** | Tourism, textiles, agricultural processing, tobacco, light manufacturing |
| **Major Imports** | Fuels, machinery |
| **Major Exports** | Agricultural products, fish, manufactured goods |
| **Major Trading Partners** | United States, Japan, Singapore, Germany, European Union |
| **Currency** | Baht |

# Government

| | |
|---|---|
| **Form of Government** | Constitutional monarchy |
| **Government Bodies** | National Assembly, Council of Ministers |
| **Formal Head of State** | Monarch |
| **Head of Government** | Prime minister |
| **Voting Rights** | All citizens 18 years of age and older |

# HISTORY AT A GLANCE

**11th century** A.D.    The Khmer Empire is founded in the area now called Thailand. The Thai people migrate to the area from China.

**13th century**    King Mengrai, the first known king of Thailand, founds the cities of Chiang Mai and Chiang Rai. He also introduces the Buddhist religion to the area.

**1280-1317**    The reign of King Ramkamhaeng is often called the golden age of Thailand. The arts and sciences flourish and the Thai alphabet comes into being.

**14th-16th centuries**    The capital city of Sukhothai goes into decline and a new capital is chosen farther away from the threats of the Burmese across the border. The new capital is Ayutthaya. The various kings of this time gradually increase their territory and begin to view themselves as almost gods.

**17th century**    Ayutthaya is a prosperous city with beautiful palaces and temples. Regular trade with China and Europe is established.

**late 17th century**    Many Thais begin to resent the European influence and Europeans are almost completely banned from the country. This ban would last almost 150 years.

**1763-1767**  War breaks out between the Thais and the Burmese. Fierce battles are fought and the Burmese eventually capture and completely destroy the capital city of Ayutthaya.

**1767**  General Taksin recaptures the destroyed city but the decision is made to move the site of the capital further south. The new capital is named Thonburi near present-day Bangkok.

**1767-1782**  Taksin is crowned king but eventually is thought to be insane and executed. General Chakri assumes the throne and takes the name King Rama I, beginning the Chakri dynasty.

**1782**  The capital city is again moved, this time to the present-day sight of Bangkok.

**1809-1824**  King Rama II reopens the borders to Europeans and allows for the exchange of ideas and trade between Thailand and the West.

**1851-1868**  King Rama IV (the king portrayed in the famous musical *The King and I*) increases the knowledge of, and communication with, western cultures.

**1868-1910**  Rama V is king for over 40 years. He does much towards the modernization of the country–abolishes slavery, sets up schools, opens a museum and national library, and starts a postal system.

**1914-1918**  King Rama VI sends Thai troops to France to fight with the Allies against the Germans in World War I.

**1920s**  Thailand joins the League of Nations, the precursor of the United Nations.

| | |
|---|---|
| **1932** | A coup d'etat forces the king to give up absolute rule and agree to a new constitution limiting his powers and making the country a constitutional monarchy. The king eventually abdicates rather than live under the new system. |
| **1939** | The countries name is officially changed from Siam to Thailand. King Rama VIII (Ananda), a 10-year-old boy ascends the throne. |
| **1939-1945** | Thailand declares its neutrality in World War II, but is attacked by Japan and forced to side with them against the Allies. An underground resistance movement begins. |
| **1946** | King Bhumibol (Rama IX) comes to the throne. Over the next three years there are a series of parliamentary governments and political instability. |
| **1950s-1960s** | The military's influence in the country increases under the command of General Pibul. Newspapers are threatened, critics of the government disappear. The king remains the one steady force in years of changing governments and oppression. |
| **late 1960s** | War rages in neighboring Vietnam. Thailand sides with South Vietnam and the United States. America funds the building of roads and air bases in Thailand and uses it as a base for planes taking off for bombing missions in Vietnam. |
| **1969** | The military-run government issues a new constitution that allows for elections to the parliament. |
| **1971-1977** | The military government again cracks down dissolving parliament. Student demonstrations even- |

tually are violently put down which mobilizes the rest of the country to rise in protest. Universities continue to lead the protests against government oppressions over the next few years.

**1977-1997**  During these two decades two military governments lead the country in a somewhat more moderate manner, but clashes between the military and student demonstrators continue. Thailand's economy is one of the fastest growing in the world with Japanese and American companies investing in the area.

**1992**  General Krapayoon declares himself prime minister without an election and the country rises up in protest. One of the larger protests is put down violently, many of the demonstrators are killed.

**1996**  King Bhumibol celebrates his golden jubilee of 50 years on the throne.

**1996-1997**  The economic corruption in the country becomes more and more evident. The economy eventually comes to a halt and a whole new restructuring is necessary.

# 1

# The Land and the People

Thailand has been called the "Land of Smiles," and on the whole the Thais have good reason to be happy. With large agricultural and mineral resources, Thailand is far more prosperous than many nations in the Far East. The country is situated in the center of Southeast Asia and covers about 198,000 square miles (over 513,000 square kilometers). Although Thailand is more than twice the size of the British Isles, and just a little smaller than France, it has a population of only 60 million. It is not, therefore, densely populated but the number of inhabitants is growing at a rate of 1 percent a year.

Thailand is shaped rather like an axe with the handle pointing south. It is bordered by Myanmar (Burma) on the north and west, by Laos on the north and northeast, by Cambodia on the east, and by Malaysia on the south. The Mekong River forms part of the border between Laos and Thailand.

The central area of Thailand consists of a low, flat plain. This plain is crisscrossed by innumerable rivers and canals, and is the

**The "Golden Triangle," where Thailand, Burma, and Laos meet.**

most fertile area of the country. The northeastern region forms a high arid plateau, while the north and the extreme south are both mountainous. The highest peak is Doi Inthanon at about 8,500 feet (2,600 meters).

Thailand's climate is tropical and very humid. There are three seasons: hot (March to May), rainy (June to October), and cool (November to February). In the hot season the average temperature is about 90 degrees Fahrenheit (32 degrees Celsius). It often reaches 102 degrees Fahrenheit (37 degrees Celsius) in April, and even in the so-called "cool" season the average temperature is still about 75 degrees Fahrenheit (25 degrees Celsius).

The people of Thailand, the Thais, originally came from the Yangtze Valley of China. They are said to have founded an empire there as early as 650 A.D. Over the centuries they were increasingly persecuted by the Chinese, and by about the 13th century A.D. they had nearly all moved south into what is now called Thailand.

Although most of the people now living in Thailand are Thais, there are also about one million Malaysians, living mainly in the south of the country near the Malaysian border.

Thailand was known as Siam until just before the Second World War. Then the Thais decided to call their country "Thailand," which can be translated as "Land of the Free." This country is the only one in Southeast Asia which has never been a colony or dominion of any other country.

Thailand is a constitutional monarchy. This means that the king is the head of state, but that a National Assembly assists the king in his ruling of the country. The National Assembly in Thailand is divided into two houses—the Senate and the House of Representatives. The 270 members of the Senate are appointed by the king for a term of six years, and they must not be under 35 years of age or members of any political party. The 393 members of the House of Representatives are elected by the Thai people and serve for four years. The members must be at least 25 years of age. If a vacancy occurs, through death or retirement, a new member can be elected but only for the rest of the four-year term. All Thais age 18 and over have the right to vote in elections.

The capital of Thailand is generally known as Bangkok. This name comes from *Bang Kok* meaning "the village of olives." Its official name, however, is *Krung Thep Mana Nakhon*, which is abbreviated in the Thai language to *Kaw Thaw Maw*. It is a sprawling

15

**Flooding is common during the rainy season. This photograph shows a flooded street in Bangkok, Thailand's capital city.**

metropolis of over 8,000,000 people—by far the largest city in Thailand. Most of Bangkok stands on the east bank of the Chao Phraya River but its industrial area is largely situated on the west bank, in the Thonburi district. Bangkok is also Thailand's most important port, in spite of the fact that it is situated 22 miles (35 kilometers) up river from the sea.

The third largest city in Thailand is Chiang Mai. Its name means "the new city," although it was founded several hundred years ago in the mid-13th century. Chiang Mai is situated about 1,000 feet (300 meters) above sea level. It is in the most mountainous part of the country, right in the middle of Thailand's great teak forests.

16

Thailand has a working population of about 32 million people. More than 50 percent work in farming and fishing, and nearly 15 percent are employed in manufacturing trades. However, the country's most rapidly growing industry is tourism. This employs well over one million people, mostly in Bangkok and Pattaya, one of the country's leading seaside resort. Tourism is now growing very quickly and, after agricultural products, is Thailand's second largest source of foreign income.

Thailand has more than 100,000 different wild flowers. These include both herbaceous and perennial plants, and a wide variety of creepers. There are also countless different types of wild orchids, as well as ferns and bamboos.

Thailand also has two main types of forest. There is the ever-

**A view of the beach at Pattaya, Thailand's leading seaside resort. Water sports are a popular attraction.**

green forest, which accounts for 30 percent of the forest area, and consists of tropical evergreen, hill evergreen, and mangrove. Then there is the deciduous forest. This accounts for the remaining 70 percent of the forest area. Teak, one of Thailand's main exports, is a deciduous tree which grows in these vast forest areas.

There are 287 different species of mammals in Thailand. Most of the larger ones belong to the forests, and can now only be seen in the national parks. These include elephants, tigers (once abundant all over Thailand), rhinoceroses, hog deers, wild buffalos, and various types of wild ox, including koupreys, gaurs, and gayals.

There are also many smaller animals. These can still occasionally be found roaming wild in many parts of the country. They include bears, deers, tapirs, gibbons, squirrels, macaques, tree shrews, weasels, and scaly anteaters (pangolins).

Thailand is also rich in many different types of birds. In fact, no fewer than 900 different species have been recorded. Among the most common are pheasants, pigeons, minivets, hornbills, barbets, hawks, parrots, kingfishers, mynahs, and various kinds of storks.

About 95 percent of Thais are Buddhists. Buddhism was probably introduced into the country by King Mengrai in the 13th century A.D. It is the national religion of Thailand and the king is the "Defender of the Faith." One of the features of Thailand is its many Buddhist temples and shrines. These usually contain a statue of the Buddha sitting in a cross-legged position. Officially, dates in Thailand are calculated in relation to the year in which the Buddha was born (543 B.C.), just as we calculate our years in

**A fertile agricultural area in northern Thailand.**

relation to the year in which Jesus Christ was born. But, in business nowadays, most people use the western calender.

The Thai language is spoken almost everywhere in the country, but there are many dialects, especially in the more rural areas. Several other languages are also widely used, such as English, Lao in the northeast, Malay in the south, and Tiechew (a dialect of Chinese) in many different parts of the country. To western ears, Thai is a very strange-sounding language. Words can have up to five different meanings, depending on the pitch and tone used in speaking. The written language was invented toward the end of the 13th century and has 44 consonants, plus dozens of vowels and tone marks.

19

# 2

# Ancient Times

Some archaeological remains found in Thailand are more than 5,000 years old. But they were not left behind by the people known as Thais. They are probably the relics of some Bronze Age community, who lived in the north of the country.

The first recorded inhabitants of Thailand, known as the Khmers, are thought to have settled in the north of the country in the 11th century A.D. But soon afterward the Thais began to move south from China. By the early 13th century a Thai, King Mengrai, and his followers had overrun almost the whole of the north. King Mengrai (the first Thai ruler known to us by name) is said to have founded the two cities of Chiang Mai and Chiang Rai. It is believed that he introduced the Buddhist religion into Thailand—a religion which was already quite widespread in India. King Mengrai also seems to have encouraged the Thais to move further and further south. By the time he died, at the age of 80, the Thais were probably firmly established over almost all of present-day Thailand.

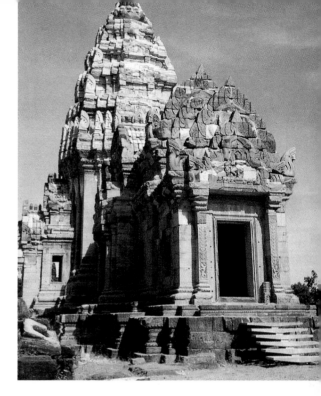

**This building, dating from the 12th century, was built by the Khmers—the first recorded inhabitants of Thailand.**

The next great ruler of Thailand was known as King Ramkamhaeng the Great, and his capital was a city called Sukhothai. He reigned from about 1280 to about 1317. King Ramkamhaeng introduced many new ideas to the country, both in the arts and the sciences. He also invented the Thai alphabet, basing it on the one used in southern India.

After King Ramkamhaeng died, Sukhothai began to decline. The Burmese were constantly invading it, and by the late 14th century the Thais had decided to abandon it. They established a new capital, much further away from the Burmese border, which they called Ayutthaya. It was only about 40 miles (65 kilometers) north of present-day Bangkok.

**The ruins of Sukothai, the capital of King Ramkamhaeng the Great.**

At about this time, the kings of Thailand began to regard themselves not just as kings but almost gods. Perhaps this was considered a useful means of maintaining power over the people in the more remote areas of the country. Although the king was considered divine, he was not allowed to be a tyrant. It was clearly understood that he only held his high office by the consent and will of the people. In fact, several kings of this period were overthrown because they were not thought to be acting for the benefit and happiness of their subjects.

By the 17th century Ayutthaya probably had a population of

almost one million, and was larger than a great many of the European capitals at that time. It was a wealthy and charmingly exotic city, with palaces, temples, and bridges—all built in a graceful and unusual style.

By then Thailand had regular contact with several European countries and a number of people from the West were even given places at court. However, this caused much unrest among the Thais, and from the end of the 17th century Europeans were almost completely banned from the country for 150 years.

But there was one Western innovation which was clearly valuable—the new, up-to-date artillery weapons which were by then quite freely available in Europe. Up to this time, the Thai troops had usually been mounted on elephants and armed only with

**A huge statue of the Buddha in the ruins of Sukothai.**

arrows or spears. But with these new weapons they believed that even on foot they would be much more successful in battle.

Over the years, the Thais had fought countless skirmishes and minor battles against their bitter enemies, the Burmese. But it was between 1763 and 1767 that the fiercest fighting took place and, despite all the Thais's modern weapons, the Burmese finally captured Ayutthaya. When the Thais later won it back they found the city merely a smouldering ruin. So their commander, Taksin, marched south and founded a new capital at a place called Thonburi. Taksin was then crowned king of Thailand. He reigned until 1782, when he was executed—because the people said he was mad.

After King Taksin's execution, General Phya Chakri came to power. He took the name of King Rama I, after a legendary Thai hero, and founded the Chakri dynasty which is still on the throne of Thailand today.

As the royal residence at Thonburi was too small, the king

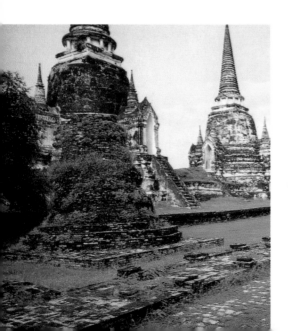

A view of some of the *chedis*, or pagodas, in Ayutthaya. Ayutthaya was the capital of Thailand for about 400 years, until the late 18th century.

**Part of the royal palace founded by King Rama I.**

decided to build a larger palace on the other side of the Chao Phraya River. This was in a tiny village called Bangkok–which thus became the fourth and greatest capital in the long history of Thailand.

King Rama I was followed by his son, King Rama II. Then came his son, King Rama III, who ruled from 1824 to 1851. During King Rama II's reign, Europeans were allowed back into the country and western influences began to spread there once more.

The next monarch, King Rama IV, was a well-respected ruler in Thailand. Unfortunately, most people outside Thailand know him only as a bad-tempered, shortsighted king portrayed in the musical and film *The King and I*. But he was, in fact, a highly educated man, who spoke seven languages and sent diplomats as far afield as England and France.

The ruler who followed, King Rama V, brought Thailand into the 20th century. He abolished slavery, and set up schools, a museum, a national library, and Thailand's first post office. His death in 1910 was a great loss to the country.

# 3

# Later Times

After 1917, Thailand gradually became more involved in European affairs. King Rama VI had been educated at Cambridge, and when the First World War broke out he sent Thai troops to France to fight side by side with the British and Commonwealth forces. After the war, Thailand joined the League of Nations, a forerunner of the United Nations. (These organizations were both set up to try to keep world peace.)

By this time, many princes, courtiers, and some sons of rich merchants were being educated in Europe. There they saw how a country could be ruled democratically, and some of them began to criticize their own country's system of government. Although capable ministers and officials were now being given powers by the king, many people thought the change was not taking place quickly enough. As a result there was a bloodless revolution in Thailand in 1932. King Rama VII was forced to agree to a new constitution, limiting his powers and making the country a democracy. However, the king never really adjusted to this new idea, and he abdicated a few years later.

**The famous bridge over the River Kwai built by prisoners of the Japanese during the Second World War.**

The next ruler of Thailand, King Rama VIII, was only a boy of ten when he came to the throne, and of course could not assume any real powers. In 1946, before he was able to take over the reins of office, he was mysteriously shot dead in his bed at the age of 20.

When the Second World War broke out, Thailand at once declared its neutrality. But, in December 1940, the Japanese asked permission to pass through Thailand to attack Malaya and Burma. The Thais refused, but the Japanese immediately attacked them and there was little the Thais could do but give in.

The Japanese then forced the Thais to declare war on the Allies.

But the sympathy of most of the Thais was with Britain and the United States. Later the Allies made a few bombing raids on Thailand, but not a great many, as Thailand had little strategic significance.

Thailand's present ruler, King Bhumibol, Rama IX, came to the throne in 1946 on the death of his brother. But because he was only 18 years old and still at a university in Switzerland, King Bhumibol was not actually crowned until May, 1950.

This king has finally brought a measure of stability to Thailand. Although there have still been a number of revolts and uprisings, King Bhumibol is very popular with the Thai people. Many people regard him as being almost a god. A picture of the king, sometimes with other members of the royal family, hangs in almost every home, shop, and factory. He is always greeted enthusiastically by throngs of people wherever he travels. When he was crowned he swore to "reign with righteousness for the benefit and happiness of all the people of Thailand," and he has obviously done his best to carry out this oath.

The king has always taken an active interest in new projects which will benefit his country. For example, he took the initiative in devising an artificial method of rainmaking so that crops would grow in the more arid regions. He has also encouraged the digging of drainage canals to help areas damaged by flooding, and has started projects to reclaim swamp land for housing or farming.

The king never forgets that he is the Defender of the Buddhist Faith in Thailand. When he was a young man, King Bhumibol became a Buddhist monk for a time, as do nearly all young men in Thailand. In his speeches he frequently quotes from the Buddhist scriptures, and he makes it clear that he aims to rule the country in keeping with his religious beliefs.

King Bhumibol also has one rather unexpected accomplishment, however. He is internationally recognized as a very talented jazz musician and composer. The Thai people are very proud of this, although jazz is not particularly popular in Thailand. (The older people mostly prefer traditional Eastern music, and the younger people like the same pop music as Western teenagers.)

In 1950 King Bhumibol married the beautiful young Queen Sirikit. Like the king, Queen Sirikit is a direct descendant of King Rama V. As a child she spent a long time in Europe, including London where her father was the Thai ambassador, and she speaks English fluently.

The queen's royal duties involve visiting children as well as the sick and the old. She is particularly interested in people who live in the more remote areas of the country. In 1979 the United Nations presented the queen with a special medal only given to women "who by their lives and their work have helped to uplift the status of women, particularly in rural areas," in recognition of their efforts.

The queen has also set up a scheme to teach handicraft skills in rural farming communities. The queen's own staff often train young people who are then able to teach others. The type of work varies from place to place, but around Chiang Mai embroidery and weaving have been very successful, as has silk production in the extreme northeast.

**Thailand is famous for the beautiful silk fabrics it produces. These girls are spinning the silk thread.**

The king and queen have four children, three girls and a boy. The heir to the throne is Crown Prince Maha Vajiralongkorn, who was born in Bangkok in 1952.

1982 marked the 200th anniversary of the crowning of the first Chakri ruler, King Rama I. This was celebrated all over the country, but particularly in Bangkok—because King Rama I had decided to make his capital there. In 1996 King Bhumibol celebrated his golden jubilee of 50 years on the throne. He is the longest-reigning monarch in the world.

# 4

# Buddhism

No one can spend long in Thailand without seeing a Buddhist monk. They wear long, saffron-colored robes covering all but their right shoulders. Most of them are aged between 17 and 22, though they vary from boys of 10 to old men. All young men are expected to spend any where from seven days to six months in a monastery. This is not compulsory, but people would think it rather odd if any young man did not want to do this. Because monks have to shave their heads, most young men decide to go into a monastery directly after their military service (which is compulsory by law) while they still have short hair!

There are also a few Buddhist nuns in Thailand. They wear white robes similar in design to the men's, and have their hair short but not shaved off altogether. Nearly all the nuns are widows who have decided, after the death of their husbands, to dedicate the rest of their lives to serving in the temples.

The founder of Buddhism, Gautama Siddartha, was born in India in about 500 B.C. He is said to have been a prince, and to

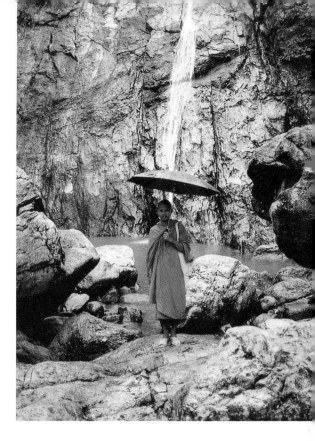

**A Buddhist monk, wearing his traditional saffron-colored robes.**

have had a luxurious childhood. Later he spent many years meditating in the countryside, and when he returned to the city he began preaching a new way of living.

Before long he was called the Buddha, which means "the enlightened one." He did not lay down any definite rules or creeds but put forward three very important ideas. The first was that violence of all kinds should be avoided, the second that people should not give way to their own selfish desires, and the third that death was not the end of a person's existence. In fact, Buddhism

33

is based on a belief in reincarnation. It teaches people that they may live a great many lives and that if they commit sins in one life they may return as an animal instead of a human being in the next. The ultimate aim is to reach the state of perfect knowledge and happiness, called Nirvana, which is a kind of heaven. Everyone can achieve this, provided he or she has followed all the Buddha's teachings as faithfully as possible in every way.

Buddhism originally became popular in India, as a reaction against the complicated Hindu religion. Many people did not like the strict class barriers and rituals of Hinduism, and found Buddhist thinking more tolerant and kind. Nowadays, however, Buddhism has almost died out in India, and Thailand is one of the few countries in the world where it is still the national religion.

At first light every morning, the Buddhist monks set off with their begging bowls to the nearest houses. They are never allowed to handle money, so the only way they can eat is to beg for food. Most people are pleased to give them something, as Buddhism teaches that they are conferring a favor on the householders by allowing them to give food to the monastery.

About midday the monks return to their monastery for their one meal of the day. After this they usually spend the rest of their time reading and meditating inside the monastery walls. They are not normally forced to stay entirely inside the monastery, and can go for walks or visit friends or relatives.

The monastery is usually built around the edge of the temple (*wat*) grounds. This is where the monks live, eat and sleep. There may also be a cloister-like area, sometimes with a number of small

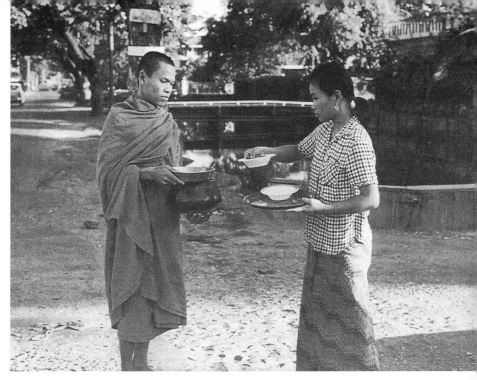

**A Thai housewife, giving food to a Buddhist monk.**

statues of the Buddha, where people can sit; and sometimes there are gardens with trees and grass, or even a small stream.

Inside the temple itself there is always a large statue of the Buddha. It usually shows him sitting cross-legged, and is nearly always brightly gilded. Sometimes the statue is also covered with tiny pieces of gold leaf which people buy to stick on it, either as a form of worship or possibly to pray for some particular favor.

Whatever the time of day there are nearly always people in the temples. They come to say a prayer or light a joss stick, but they do not usually stay very long. When the monks meet together

35

**Worshippers in a Buddhist temple. Whatever the time of day, there are nearly always people in the temples—an indication of the importance of religion in everyday life for the Thais.**

several times a day to chant and pray, the visitors do not join in the prayers but continue with their own private worship.

There is also a curious rattling sound in nearly all Buddhist temples. This is made by people shaking a long, cylindrical wooden box, filled with 30 or 40 wooden spills. Once a spill has been shaken out the person takes it to an attendant who reads the number on the side of the spill, and then hands over a sheet of paper covered with writing. This paper is supposed to tell the person's future. It may say that a business transaction will turn out well, or that the person will meet a dark, handsome stranger! After reading it, the person takes two larger sticks with special markings on them and throws them up in the air. If they both land the same way up it is a sign that the prediction will come true, but if they land on different sides then the outcome is not so certain.

Visitors to some Buddhist temples have to take off their shoes. This is partly a sign of respect and partly to keep the dust from the streets out of the temple. Also, in all Buddhist temples it is strictly forbidden to sit on the ground with one's feet pointing toward the altar, as this shows disrespect to the Buddha—so feet must always be tucked under the body.

One sign of the strength of the Buddhist religion in Thailand is all the tiny shrines. These are found in the gardens of private

**Tiny shrines such as this can be seen all over Thailand—even outside factories and in gas station forecourts.**

houses and hotels, and even in garage entrances and at the entrance to factories. A typical shrine looks rather like a doll's house on the top of a pole. Inside there is a small statue of the Buddha, with incense sticks, flowers, or perhaps small offerings of food in front of it.

Buddhism is quite tolerant of other religious faiths. There is never any ill-feeling shown by Buddhists to the Hindu Indians who live in Thailand, or to the Malaysians who are Muslims. This is because Buddhism tries to show people how they should live, rather than teaching that certain beliefs are right and that all other beliefs are therefore wrong.

# 5

# Bangkok

Bangkok was only a small fishing village until King Rama I decided to make it his capital in 1782. There was unlimited space to build a magnificent palace there, and the king thought he would be safer from his enemies, the Burmese, on the east side of the wide Chao Phraya River.

For tourists, one of Bangkok's main attractions is the Grand Palace. This is not just one palace, but a whole group of royal residences, temples, museums, and offices. Sometimes described as a city within a city, its numerous buildings are crowded together inside a white wall more than one mile (nearly two kilometers) long.

The first four kings of the Chakri dynasty lived their entire lives within the walls of the palace. They were thought to be far too important to mix with ordinary people. Each king added new buildings, mainly in the traditional Thai style, with steeply sloping tiled roofs. However, there are also a few buildings in European style.

Three of the buildings in the Grand Palace are particularly fine.

One is the magnificent Throne Hall, built in the reign of King Rama V. Here the king is crowned, while seated on the coronation chair under a nine-tiered white canopy. Then there is the Audience Hall of Amarindra, which also has a throne with a nine-tiered white canopy, as well as a golden boat-shaped altar. Finally there is the Audience Hall of Dusit Maha Prasad. This is a perfect example of a classical Thai palace, with its roof rising in four tiers and topped by a slim gilt spire.

**Wat Phra Keo, one of the temples in the Grand Palace. This temple contains the famous "Emerald Buddha," a small statue made of jasper.**

There are also a number of temples, or *wats*, in the Grand Palace. One of them, Wat Phra Keo, contains one of Thailand's most highly-prized religious images—the "Emerald Buddha." It is actually made of jasper and is only about two feet (60 centimeters) tall, but looks very imposing on top of its high golden altar. An interesting custom with this Buddha is that its clothes are changed with the seasons. In the hot season it wears thin robes, in the rainy season slightly thicker ones and in the cool season the thickest of all. Europeans may find this odd (especially because it is hot in Thailand even in the so-called cool season!) but it is a tradition that dates back to the very early days of the Chakri dynasty.

There are at least 300 other *wats* in Bangkok. The oldest and largest is Wat Pho, which was founded in the 16th century when Bangkok was still only a village. Inside the temple is a huge statue of the Buddha, lying on its side. This statue is 150 feet (46 meters) long and 50 feet (15 meters) high.

Wat Arun stands on the far side of the river in Thonburi. It is covered all over with tiny pieces of shining pottery. The name *Wat Arun* means "Temple of the Dawn," and when the sun shines in the early morning it sparkles and looks quite magical.

Wat Saket stands on top of a high mound, and from the top there is a wonderful view all over Bangkok. But the Thai people do not climb it for the view. They go to visit the shrine, which is supposed to contain many small relics of the Buddha which were sent there from India.

Wat Trimitr is famous for its solid gold Buddha. This was only discovered in 1953 when a heavy clay Buddha was being moved

A view of Bangkok, taken from Wat Saket.

by a crane. The statue was dropped and broke open to reveal the
gold Buddha inside. Weighing five and a half tons, the Buddha is
700-800 years old. It was probably covered with clay to prevent it
being stolen by Burmese invaders.

Not far from the Grand Palace is the Pramane Ground. This is
an immense open space, where a huge market with more than
10,000 stalls is held every Saturday and Sunday. Everything seems
to be on sale there, from gleaming ceremonial swords, to shirts
and jeans, white mice dyed green, and even a large variety of cats
(including some Siamese cats).

The building boom in recent years has seen towering glass buildings replacing many of the long stretches of two-, three- and four-story buildings. Bangkok is a large, straggling city, with no real center, although there are several areas which are extremely busy and important.

When Bangkok was first founded it had almost no roads. Instead, the whole city was crisscrossed by canals, or *klongs*, as they are called. The inhabitants of the city lived by the side of these klongs, and everything they needed was brought to them in wide, flat-bottomed barges. Then, in the 1860s, the "New Road" was built. Today this is still one of the main routes through the city and a major business area. A large number of European firms have offices there, as well as many important Thai firms. As time went on, most of the klongs were filled in and replaced by roads, and today Bangkok has some of the noisiest and busiest streets in the world.

Another well-known street in Bangkok is Ratchadamnoen Nok. It is a wide leafy avenue, with the Democracy Monument at one end. It is lined on both sides with government offices, many of them having the same steep roofs that are found on all traditional-style Thai temples and palaces.

One reminder of Bangkok's past is the famous floating market. Every morning, the moment it becomes light, dozens of small boats (laden with everything from fish to vegetables) meet on a canal just outside the city. In recent years, however, the floating market has become much smaller. The only way to get some idea of what it was once like is to visit another floating market at Damnoen Saduak, about two hours' drive to the southwest.

Another relic of the past are the royal barges. When Bangkok had no roads the kings had to use these barges for all ceremonial occasions. Today 30 of these ornate, gilded boats are on show in the royal boatyards. The largest and most graceful (which needs 60 oarsmen to row it) is still used for special state processions.

The Red Cross Snake Farm is one of the most unusual places in Bangkok. Dozens of gaily patterned cobras, spotted vipers, and banded kraits (a dangerous Indian snake) are kept here, along

**The solid gold Buddha in Wat Trimitr, discovered in 1953. This statue weighs five and a half tons and is over 700 years old.**

**The royal barges—ornate gilded boats—on show in the royal boatyards. The largest is still used for some state processions.**

with numerous other poisonous snakes. Visitors can come and see the snakes being milked of their venom. This is then processed to provide anti-snakebite serum for use all over Southeast Asia.

# 6

# Other Cities and Towns

Thailand's third largest city, Chiang Mai, is about 400 miles (640 kilometers) north of Bangkok. It stands on a plateau surrounded by some of Thailand's highest and most densely wooded mountains. It is a pleasant place, with far less noise and bustle than Bangkok and, being so high, there is almost perfect spring-like weather from October to January.

Originally Chiang Mai was surrounded by a huge city wall. It is said that King Mengrai the Great ordered it to be built in the 13th century. It took 90,000 men, working shifts all round the clock, several months to complete it; and much of the wall can still be seen round the old part of the city today.

King Mengrai probably also founded the temple called Wat Chiang Mai. This contains the Crystal Buddha and the Marble Buddha. Another temple is Wat Doi Suthep, which stands on the side of a steep hill just outside the city, some 3,400 feet (1,100 meters) above sea level. Three hundred steps, with stone serpents on either side, lead up to it; but visitors are rewarded for the

**Making lacquerware bowls in Chiang Mai. Each craft is concentrated in one area of the city, where the craftsmen live and work.**

climb not only by the sight of hundreds of images of the Buddha but also by a superb view over the city.

Like European craftsmen in the Middle Ages, the craftsmen in Chiang Mai live in groups. For example, all the silversmiths live in one district, hammering delicate patterns on bowls and trays all day long. There is also a district for the lacquerware workers, who use strands of colored straw to decorate boxes and bowls, as well as areas where the woodcarvers and the furniture makers live. Perhaps the most fascinating craft to watch is the umbrella-making. This is the traditional craft for village girls in Bor Sang, a little way east of Chiang Mai. A girl takes a length of bamboo and adds thin wooden spokes and a thin paper covering. Then

**A young Thai girl, painting designs on paper umbrellas. This is a traditional craft practiced by girls in the village of Bor Sang, near Chiang Mai.**

she paints designs on the umbrella. Sometimes the customers even tell her what designs they would like!

The king of Thailand has his country home in Chiang Mai. He and the rest of the royal family spend several months there every year to escape the heat and bustle of Bangkok. When the king is not in residence, the palace grounds are open to visitors. They can walk through the beautiful gardens and see the flowers which have been brought from many parts of the world.

48

A city with a similar name, Chiang Rai, is the provincial capital of northern Thailand. Like Chiang Mai, it was founded in the 13th century by King Mengrai. According to legend, the king's elephant escaped and led him to a spot near the Mekong River. The king decided to build a city there, partly because of the beauty of the site and partly because of its strategic position. Today Chiang Rai looks rather like a town in the midwest of America, because the present-day town was laid out by an American missionary. It has some interesting old Buddhist temples, built on hilltops just outside Chiang Rai itself, from which there are pleasant views of both the town and the river.

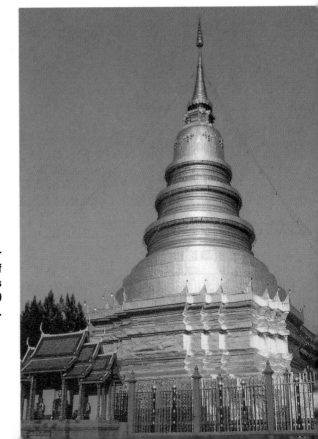

The huge gold *chedi*, or pagoda, in the middle of Lamphun monastery. It is probably more than 1,000 years old.

Lamphu, also in the north, is best known for its beautiful fabrics. It also has an ancient monastery, which is always crowded with people studying or meditating. The huge gold *chedi*, or pagoda, in the middle of the monastery was probably begun more than 1,000 years ago, before the Thai people themselves arrived in the country.

Only 100 miles (160 kilometers) north of Bangkok is Lop Buri which, in the 17th century, was considered second only to the capital, Ayutthaya. In Lop Buri there are the remains of a royal palace which must have been very imposing when it was first built. One feature of the palace is the many small niches in its high walls, in which lighted candles are placed during festivals. One of the many ancient shrines in the city is dedicated to a Hindu deity and houses a large troop of friendly monkeys. Visitors often buy a bunch of bananas to give the monkeys as they run around the shrine, but unfortunately the monkeys sometimes seem to think it is fun to steal the visitor's cameras or handbags!

Kanchanaburi is only a short distance from the famous bridge over the Kwai River. Near the bridge is a cemetery where more than 8,000 soldiers are buried. They were prisoners of war in Thailand under the Japanese, and died building the bridge and the railway. The bridge is constructed of huge iron girders. It is still used by trains two or three times a day, as well as by pedestrians and cyclists—who apparently know exactly when the next train is due.

Southeast of Kanchanaburi is Nakhon Pathom, the oldest city in Thailand. It has the tallest temple in the country, some 395 feet

(100 meters) high. This was begun in the mid-19th century, and has a vast gold-tiled dome, inside which are the remains of a much older temple, built around 150 A.D.

Phuket is the best-known city in the south of Thailand. It stands on Thailand's biggest island, linked to the rest of the country by a causeway. Many tourists visit Phuket because of its fine white sand and clear sea. (The Thais themselves cannot understand why foreigners enjoy sunbathing and swimming!) The sea all along the coast of Thailand is full of fascinating coral and brilliantly colored fish, and underwater diving is a popular way for tourists to explore the variety of life below the seas surface. People who are less energetic or not so good at swimming can hire a glass-bottomed boat and view things in a more leisurely way. Unfortunately, due to pollution, there is not as much to see as there used to be.

Another busy place in the extreme south is called Hat Yai. This town is only about 30 miles (50 kilometers) from the Malaysian border, and does a good trade in smuggling. It is also well-known for its bullfights. In Thailand this does not mean a bullfighter trying to kill a bull (as in Spain). Here, two specially-trained bulls fight each other until one becomes tired and ambles away.

# 7

# The Klong People and the Hill Tribes

At one time *klongs*, or canals, were found almost everywhere in Thailand. But over the years many of them have been filled in and replaced by roads, especially those in Bangkok. However there are still large numbers of people who make their homes

**A typical klong-dweller's home.**

**The famous floating market at Damnoen Saduak—note the women's traditional lampshade-shaped hats.**

beside the klongs, and who live their lives almost entirely around the water.

The homes of these klong dwellers are wooden houses built on piles. A typical house has just one floor, with an overhanging roof, and a short wooden pier where a boat can be tied up. The klong dwellers spend nearly all their time outdoors. They use the klong for everything from washing themselves to washing their clothes.

Some of the klong dwellers cultivate a small piece of land behind their homes. Others work in the many timber yards found beside most of the klongs or run small shops or restaurants. Klong dwellers may also run garages, supplying gas for the outboard motors of the long narrow boats, called *sampans*.

The klongs are at their liveliest first thing in the morning. From about half past five onward, hundreds of sampans, all laden with produce, meet together at one or other of Thailand's famous floating markets. The best-known of all is held in Thonburi (Bangkok's industrial district), but by far the busiest and most exciting takes place at Damnoen Saduak, about 60 miles (110 kilometers) to the west.

Usually the woman in the family takes the goods to market. Dressed in traditional Thai clothes, with a hat like a wide straw lampshade, she not only steers the boat but also serves the customers. Most of the goods for sale are produced by the klong people themselves, and are mainly such things as watermelons, bananas, and pineapples. Fish, meat, and various household utensils are also on sale. There are always a number of floating cafes at the markets, selling tea, coffee, and various canned drinks. It all makes a very colorful, exciting spectacle, and hundreds of visitors come every morning to watch, viewing it either from motorboats or from one of the many small footbridges that cross the canals.

From time to time the canals have to be cleaned out. Then a householder will build two mud walls, one on either side of his house across the water. The thick, evil-smelling silt is lifted out of the canal by hand, put on carts, and taken to the rice fields to be used as manure.

A much more primitive people are the hill tribes who live north of Chiang Mai. They are a different race from the Thais, but no one is quite certain where they originally came from. They have a different language, religion, and way of life from the people in the rest of the country; and over the centuries have had very little contact with the rest of the population.

Some of the best known hill tribes are the Yao, the Meo, and the Akha. The Yao live only a little way north of Chiang Mai, while most of the other tribes live on the slopes of mountains at least 3,500 feet (1,100 meters) above sea level, where they believe they are safe from evil spirits.

Many of the hill tribes live today in the same way as they have

**Meo children, members of one of the northern hill tribes.**

**Yao women in their traditional red and black costumes.**

done for centuries. Their homes are rickety wooden houses on stilts, with a few pigs and dogs roaming around. The men plow the fields with the aid of water buffalos, while the women (with their babies strapped on their backs) mill the corn between two stones. In their traditional red and black costumes with beads or coins round their heads, these people look very attractive. However, the hill-tribesmen have had many problems over the years, partly because they are cut off from the rest of the world and are largely uneducated.

56

For example, the hill tribes use a "slash and burn" method of agriculture. This means that people cut down and burn parts of the huge teak forests in order to grow their crops. In the short term this produces good harvests, but within five or six years the soil is exhausted and the hill tribes have to cut down another area of trees. This is a very wasteful method of cultivation. Gradually the forests are destroyed and it will take centuries to replace them. This reduces the amount of teak that can be produced, which is a serious loss to the Thai export trade. It also causes a change in the watershed patterns, which results in flooding in the plains and disrupts the rice cultivation there.

The cultivation of the opium poppy among the hill tribes

**An Akha village in northern Thailand—note the rickety wooden houses and poor living conditions.**

reached enormous proportions in the 1980s in the "Golden Triangle" where Thailand, Myanmar (Burma), and Laos meet. Opium has been illegally exported to Europe and America, where it fetches huge sums on the "black" market. This was very worrying to the Thai government and strong measures have been introduced to deal with the problem. The possession of heroin is punishable by terms of imprisonment varying from five years to life and by exceptionally heavy fines. The possession of marijuana is punishable by anything up to six months in prison.

Perhaps most worrying of all for the Thai government in the

This land, once covered in valuable teak trees, has been cleared by burning so that the hill tribes can grow their crops. The soil will soon be exhausted and the hill tribes will have to cut down more trees.

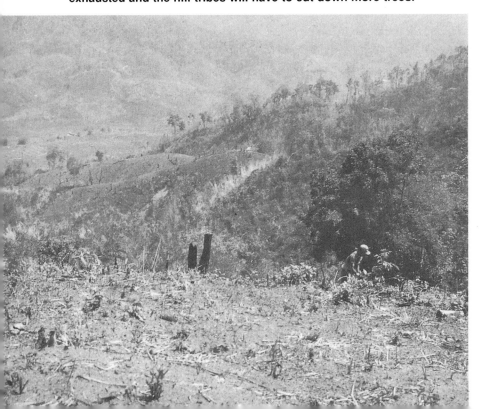

1980s was the spread of terrorist gangs among the hill tribes. These came across the border from neighboring Communist countries, particularly Laos and Vietnam. They used small hill-tribe villages as hideouts, and several times government troops had to go north to put down riots and revolts of various kinds.

The government undertook a massive education program. Agricultural experts traveled far, often on foot, to teach the hill-tribesmen about up-to-date farming methods. As a result, entire villages now grow peaches, beans, strawberries, coffee, and a special kind of rice that will grow on hillsides. This has largely put an end to the "slash and burn" farming methods. It has also slowed down the opium trade, which has never been as profitable to the Thais themselves as to the drug peddlers in the West. Volunteer teachers have set up mobile schools to teach the tribesmen to read and write, in the hope of bringing them into closer contact with the rest of the country.

# 8

# Agriculture and Industry

Thailand's wealth lies in its land—in its agriculture, forestry, fisheries, mineral resources and, more recently, in its natural gas. Approximately 35 percent of the land is under cultivation, and a large proportion of the rest is either used for animal husbandry or is forested.

The main agricultural crop in Thailand is rice. Paddy fields cover vast areas of land, and are mostly plowed by water buffalos. Rice is the staple food in Thailand. It is also one of the country's main exports and Thailand has become one of the world's biggest rice exporter. Tapioca is also grown in the east and northeast of the country. Although much of it is used for home consumption, Thailand is also one of the world's largest tapioca exporter. Maize is grown extensively in most parts of the country, with a large portion of the crop exported every year. Sugarcane is grown in many different parts of Thailand, with most of the produce being sold in Thailand. Coffee was introduced into the country but initially most of the bushes were rather immature

**Harvesting rice, Thailand's main agricultural crop.**

and it took some time to get any yield. Today there are some prospering coffee plantations in parts of the country.

In the south of Thailand the main crop is rubber. The liquid which comes from the rubber plant is called latex and half a million tons of it are produced annually. Nearly all the rubber is exported making Thailand one of the world's largest exporters with the other Asian countries of Malaysia and Indonesia.

Tobacco production has been increasing steadily in recent years and a Virginia-type tobacco is the kind that is most usually grown in Thailand. The Thai people themselves are not particularly heavy smokers, and two-thirds of the crop is exported every year.

Another very important crop is cotton. It is mostly exported in its raw state, but a certain amount is made into cloth for the home market. Jute, which is mainly used for mats or sacking, is also an important crop, and over 30,000 tons are exported every year.

Silk has been produced in Thailand for centuries. In fact, the Thais may have brought the art of silk production with them when they moved south from China. Thai silk can be made into

**These women are taking the husks off coconuts—coconuts are one of the most important crops in the south of Thailand.**

**A girl weaving silk in Chiang Mai. Thai silk is a valuable source of foreign income.**

anything from delicate blouses to heavy bedspreads and most of it is exported.

One of Thailand's best-known and most valuable products is teak. The trees mostly grow in the mountainous areas in the north, and the logs are deftly moved around by elephants. Nowadays nearly all the teak is made into furniture or ornaments of some kind, and then exported, mainly to Europe and America. In the great teak forests there is nearly always rattan, which is used for making cane furniture. Another commercial product from the forests is dammar, a resin which comes from the conifers and which is used in the manufacture of varnish and shellacs of various kinds.

Thailand ranks third in the world as a fishing nation. It has a fleet of over 40,000 fishing vessels, and an annual catch of about two million tons. The fishing boats mostly ply in the Gulf of Thailand and in the nearby South China Sea and Indian Ocean, and about half of the catch is exported.

Tin ore is by far the most important mineral deposit in Thailand. Most of the tin is found in the south of the country, near the Malaysian border. After Malaysia and Indonesia, Thailand is one of the world's largest producers of tin, which is mostly exported to the United States, Japan, and the Netherlands.

Thailand also has the world's largest deposits of potash. This is

**Working elephants near the city of Lamphun.**

**Tin mining at Phuket in the south. Tin ore is the most important mineral deposit in Thailand.**

mostly used for fertilizers in Thailand itself, and very little is exported. In addition, Thailand has deposits of gypsum, kaolin, copper, graphite, asbestos, and rock salt.

People who like fluoride in their toothpaste probably never ask where it comes from. If they did, the answer might very well be Thailand. This non-metallic ore, which is also used extensively in steel production, is exported from Thailand in large quantities, particularly to Japan, Russia, and the Netherlands.

Thailand has a large variety of precious and semi-precious stones. These include rubies, sapphires, emeralds, and topaz.

There is also a certain amount of precious metal to be found in Thailand, and most of the stones are set in locally mined gold or silver and then sold as jewelry.

Thailand's latest discovery has been natural gas. It was first tapped in the Gulf of Thailand in 1981, and several other fields are now in operation as well. The first consumer of the gas was an electricity generating plant, but it is now available for all kinds of industrial purposes.

# 9

# Education, Medicine, and Transportation

Until the late 19th century education in Thailand mainly took place in the *wats* (temples) and only boys were given any tuition. The pupils lived in the monasteries, and waited on the monks in return for their board and lessons. However, only a small number of parents sent their sons to be educated, and in any case the teaching was limited to the "three Rs" and religious and moral instruction.

The kings, however, were well aware of the value of education. King Rama III learned to speak English so that he could read English books. He set up a number of schools. He also encouraged Christian missionaries to open schools and even employed European teachers for the royal princes.

King Rama IV continued the work begun by his father. He established a school in the palace so that the sons of court officials could be educated. Many boys from this school, and the king's own sons, later went on to schools and colleges in Europe.

**Buddhist monks studying in a monastery in Bangkok. Until the late 19th century, this was virtually the only form of education available in Thailand.**

Education gradually became more and more widespread in Thailand until, in 1892, a Ministry of Education was set up. In the same year the first Teacher's Training College was opened. It was called Chulalongkorn University, in honor of King Rama V who was sometimes known as King Chulalongkorn. In 1921 a law made schooling compulsory for all children for nine years. This was difficult because of shortages of both teachers and schools, especially in the more rural areas.

Today there are five educational levels in Thailand. The first is the kindergarten, for children aged three and a half to seven, which only a small number of children attend. Then comes the elementary school, which covers the years of compulsory education. Most children leave school after this.

For the children who stay on for the third level there is a choice of three types of school. In each type of school, however, the course lasts for six years. There is a general course for those who are going to work afterward, a training course for those going on to technical colleges and an academic course for those who wish to go on to university.

Unfortunately there are not nearly enough of these secondary schools, and many children are too poor to be able to take advantage of them. Although the teaching is free, the students have to provide all their own books and materials, and the government cannot help to pay for such things as meals or traveling expenses.

Some students go on to the fourth educational level and spend two years at technical college. The first of these was opened in

**Thai schoolchildren taking part in a physical education class.**

**Pupils at a girls' secondary school in Bangkok.**

Bangkok in 1952. Today there are three similar colleges in the provinces as well, all preparing students to take jobs in engineering, agriculture, or commerce.

For other students the fourth level is a pre-university college. They have to spend two years there, which means that they are at least 22 before they can go to a university. While they are at the pre-university college they have to study at least one foreign language. This is usually English, French, or Chinese, because most textbooks in Thailand are still written in one of these languages.

The last educational level is a university. Thailand has eight

70

universities, five of which are in Bangkok. It normally takes four years to obtain a degree (six for medicine or dentistry). But a degree in agriculture or engineering takes only three years and a teacher's certificate only two.

After Chulalongkorn, the next oldest university in Thailand is Thammasat University. It is in Bangkok and was opened in 1934. Two more universities were founded in Bangkok in 1943, and the fifth, a university specializing in agricultural subjects, in 1948.

The first university founded outside Bangkok was Chiang Mai University. It was opened in 1965 in beautiful grounds on the edge of the city. This was followed by Khon Kaen University, and then by the Prince of Songkhla's University.

Education has now been compulsory in Thailand for well over 70 years, and now about 90 percent of Thais are able to read and write.

One of the problems in the south of the country was that most of the people there are Malaysians, and the children speak only Malay until they go to school. But, by law, at least 50 percent of the teaching in schools must be in Thai—so the children then have to work in two languages, which is naturally rather a handicap.

In 1950 the United Nations started to help in Thailand's education program. It launched several training schemes in rural areas to teach young people a trade. The teaching is generally about agriculture and handicrafts, as these are the occupations most suited to these areas. A typical training center is the one at Ubon, in the northeast. From here groups of teachers travel around to all the neighboring villages. They instruct young people in modern methods of agriculture and domestic science and where necessary also teach them to read and to write.

Medical care in Thailand is of a very high standard. There are well over 400 well-equipped hospitals and clinics, staffed by highly trained doctors. Unfortunately, the medical care is not free, but the government is doing its best to ensure that even the poorest people receive attention when they need it.

There are also approximately 6,500 health centers, where

**Members of the Akha hill tribe, including a young schoolgirl. Government-funded education programs are bringing the hill tribes into closer contact with their fellow countrymen.**

advice and treatment are given. Like the hospitals, they are not free, but there are usually special arrangements for the poor. These clinics are found almost everywhere in the country, although there are unfortunately still some isolated areas, such as the districts where the hill tribes live, where they do not exist.

Life expectancy in Thailand at the moment is somewhat lower than in Europe or America. It is 65 years for a man, and about 73 years for a woman. This has improved from a few years ago, now that such diseases as malaria have been largely eliminated (malaria is now found only in a few rural areas), and that the standard of nutrition is improving.

There is an excellent bus service in Bangkok and the other large towns in Thailand. The buses are extremely cheap, and there is a flat rate fare regardless of the length of the journey. A long-distance bus service links the various towns; and the buses on these routes are usually air conditioned and very comfortable. There are countless taxis in Thailand, and these are also very cheap. Air-conditioned taxis are about double the price of the others, but even they are relatively inexpensive. In addition, there are large numbers of *samlors* for hire. In country areas, this means a small three-wheeled vehicle which the driver pedals like a bicycle; but in Bangkok a motorized three-wheeled vehicle is used.

The Thailand State Railway links Bangkok with all the other major towns in the country. It also connects with services in Malaysia, which run as far as Singapore. All the trains are pulled by diesel locomotives, and together they carry over 100 million passengers and well over 10 million tons of freight every year.

Thai Airways International operates from Bangkok's Don Muang Airport. Although it was only formed in 1959, it now carries more than two million passengers every year. Its fleet of planes, with their distinctive purple and gold livery, includes 16 Airbus 300 planes and eight Boeing 747s, as well as a number of other planes.

The domestic airline, Thai Airways, connects Bangkok with all the larger towns in the country. It also connects Bangkok with Kuala Lumpur and Penang (both in Malaysia), and with the capitals of Vietnam and Laos and carries an ever-increasing number of both tourists and businessmen.

**A busy street scene in Bangkok. This photograph shows a three-wheeled samlor, one of the most common means of transportation.**

**Passengers waiting for a train at Ayutthaya station. The Thailand State Railway connects all the major towns with Bangkok.**

Many foreign airlines also use Don Muang Airport. For this reason the airport was enlarged and modernized. When the work was completed, more than 7,500 passengers were then able to use the airport every hour of the day.

# 10

# Food and Drink

The main feature of Thai food is that it is extremely spicy. In fact it is so hot that most Europeans can only eat a rather watered-down version. The hottest ingredient is a tiny red or green chili called *prik-kee-nooh*, which the Thais like to add to almost everything they prepare.

The Thais also eat a lot of steamed rice. This helps balance the spiciness of the peppers and gives bulk to the meal. The poorer people are, the more rice they tend to eat—because rice is by far the cheapest food available in Thailand.

A prosperous family may begin a meal with spring rolls—but a spicier kind than those sold in the West. The outside is a kind of delicate, crisp pancake, and inside there may be sweet and sour pork, crabmeat, bean sprouts, or almost anything else the family like to eat.

Another starter, called *gai hor bai toey*, is served in a rolled-up leaf. Although it looks different from the spring roll the ingredients inside are often much the same. There may be chunks of

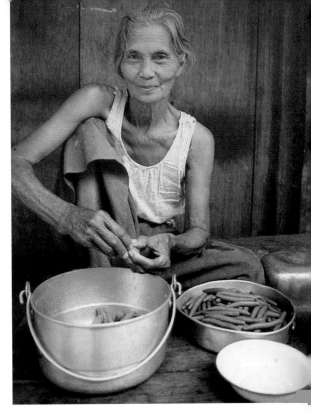

**Thai food is often very spicy. This lady is preparing a local delicacy.**

chicken fried in sesame oil, soya sauce, and oyster sauce, and extra flavor may be obtained by adding a few drops of whisky.

One of the most popular soups in Thailand is called *tom-yam-gung*. The broth is prepared with various herbs, and then pieces of chicken, fish, or prawns are added. Once the ingredients are tender, lemon juice is added, along with *prik-kee-nooh*, and the soup is always brought to the table piping hot.

Fish is eaten by almost everyone in Thailand. Sometimes it is eaten raw, but it can also be cooked in a great variety of different ways. One popular dish is baked *pladook*, which is rather like a catfish. This is cooked with cloves, nutmeg, and ginger, and served

77

**The Thais eat a lot of fruit. Fruit stalls such as this one can be seen throughout the country.**

with chili sauce. Crisp fried prawns are also popular with many Thai people. These are usually served with a choice of several different sauces. But most families will eat almost any type of fish, especially if it is fried and covered with one of their favorite sauces.

For the main course a very popular dish is *gaeng pet*. This literally means "hot curry," and it can be made with pork, chicken, beef, fish, or prawns. It has a slightly sweet taste because it is cooked in coconut milk, but it contains many different spices.

*Gai yang* is probably best described as barbecued chicken. It is one of the few Thai dishes which does not taste very different from a Western dish. A whole chicken is stuffed with grated coconut, and the chicken is then rotated on a spit over glowing charcoal. The coconut is removed before the chicken is served.

78

Desserts in Thailand usually look very attractive. However, they are often very sweet and sticky, and Westerners find them rather sickly. One of the most popular desserts is a sticky cold rice, in which the grains are dyed pretty greens and pinks, and served with tiny chips of ice.

The Thais all eat a great deal of fruit. Oranges, bananas, melons, and pineapples are all equally popular. The Thais also like *durians*, which are a kind of prickly plum. They smell just like rotten eggs, but are very sweet and juicy to eat. Mangoes are popular too, but they are only in season from March to May. Slices of mango are often served with rice cooked in coconut milk. Chilled mango, left to go nearly rotten, is also a popular dessert—especially powdered with grated ginger and poppy seeds.

Tea, coffee, and soft drinks are all popular. Thailand also produces its own beer. Wine is not drunk a great deal because it is extremely expensive; but various spirits are quite popular, especially whiskey.

Westerners are often surprised that there are no knives on the tables in Thailand. The reason for this is that the food is already cut up into small pieces before it is served. The table is normally laid with a fork on the left and a spoon on the right, although chopsticks are sometimes used with a stew.

In restaurants people are sometimes given a cold towel so that they can cool their hands and their faces. In fact, the towel is sometimes brought from the refrigerator. Similarly, better-off people nearly always have a cold face towel beside their plates on the table at home, in much the same way as Westerners might have a napkin.

**Street hawkers, selling food in Bangkok—a well-established tradition in Thailand.**

There are countless hawkers selling food in the streets in Thailand. Most of them offer a large variety of nuts, as well as slices of watermelon and pineapple. Some of them also sell meat balls and pastas stuck on skewers like kebabs so that they can be eaten in the street. Drinks of various kinds are also on sale. These include sodas and the more traditional Thai drinks, such as iced sugarcane juice, lightly spiced and scented with cinnamon and cloves, and chilled lemon or lime tea.

# 11

# Festivals

There can be few countries which have as many festivals as Thailand. They vary from small to large, and from lighthearted and amusing to solemn and religious. Most of them take place either in Bangkok or in Chiang Mai, although some are national festivals which take place nearly everywhere in the country.

A festival in January, marking the start of the western New Year, is a popular celebration. Many householders hang colored fairy lights in their gardens, the temples are decorated and there are special Thai dances and games at the Pramane Ground in Bangkok.

In February every year comes the *Magha Puja*. This reminds people of the time when the Buddha gave a sermon containing all his teaching in front of 1,250 disciples. Buddhists go to their local temple to recite special prayers and then they make a clockwise procession round the temple carrying lighted candles.

The Flower Festival in Chiang Mai is also held in February. Both temperate and tropical flowers grow in abundance in Chiang

**Visitors to the Grand Palace in Bangkok, celebrating Chakri Day, the day on which General Phya Chakri was crowned as King Rama I. They are visiting the royal temples to show their love and respect for the monarchy.**

Mai, especially in the early part of the year. A huge carnival is held, with long processions of flower-covered floats and parades traveling round the city.

April 6th every year is known as Chakri Day, because it was on this day in 1782 that General Phya Chakri was crowned as King Rama I. The main celebrations take place in the grounds of the Grand Palace in Bangkok, where thousands of people visit the royal temples, to show their love and respect for the monarchy.

April 13th is *Songkran,* the traditional Thai New Year. This is a boisterous, fun-filled time. In Bangkok the festival begins with a long procession of floats, representing all kinds of groups and organizations. There are many bands playing a variety of curious eastern instruments. Then there is a huge fair on the Pramane

82

Ground. Groups of Buddhist monks sit under a huge awning waiting for people to place gifts at their feet. There are also countless bird sellers, as setting free a caged bird is thought to bring good luck. Another traditional activity is to sprinkle water on the Buddha images, on the monks, and on any older, respected people. In recent years, however, this has tended to become mainly an amusement for children and teenagers. Instead of water they usually use a kind of thin whitewash, and they all try to see how many of their friends or even casual passersby they can splash with thin streaks of white.

The *Songkran* festival is particularly lively and colorful in Chiang Mai. This is probably because the people there are not as sophisticated or restrained as many of the modern Bangkok city dwellers. Besides processions and fairs, there is dancing in the streets, often lasting for hours, and there are beauty contests for the girls, which always attract large crowds.

In May there is the Royal Plowing Ceremony in Bangkok. This is held on a date fixed every year by the king's astrologers, to open the rice-planting season. There are several kinds of traditional ceremonies and processions on the Pramane Ground at which the king and queen are present. The whole festival is designed to ensure a good rice harvest.

Also in May is *Visakha Puja*. This commemorates the Buddha's birth, and conversion and his passing into *Nirvana*. Many temples all over the country are illuminated with thousands of paper lanterns, and there are torchlight processions and sometimes firework displays.

Then there is the *Boon Bong Fai*, or Rocket Festival. This is also held in May, mainly in the smaller towns and villages in the northeast of Thailand. The aim is to ensure a good rainy season, so that the crops will grow. However, the festival is chiefly known for its drum playing and its exciting displays of homemade fireworks.

October 23rd is King Chulalongkorn Day. This is held every year in remembrance of King Rama V, who was also called King Chulalongkorn. Thousands of people pour into Bangkok to lay wreaths of flowers at the foot of the king's statue, to show their gratitude for all that the king did for the country.

The rainy season usually ends toward the end of October. To celebrate this one of the most magnificent spectacles of the year often takes place in Bangkok. The king goes in his royal barge, accompanied by several golden barges, to Wat Arun, and gives the monks new yellow robes and various other gifts, as an offering of thanks.

Perhaps the most beautiful of all is the *Loi Krathong* festival.

**The tug-of-war at the Elephant Round-up in Surin.**

This is held on the night of the full moon in the 12th lunar month (usually early November). It has no connection with any Buddhist rites or beliefs, and is probably a survival of ancient spirit worship, when offerings were made to the water gods. People make little boats out of banana leaves, and put a candle and one or two incense sticks inside them. Alternatively, they may buy little boats, which are often in the shape of a swan or duck. Then they go to the nearest river and sing their favorite folk songs as they place the fragile craft on the water and watch them float away down the stream.

In November comes the Elephant Round-up at Surin, in northeastern Thailand. Two hundred or more elephants are rounded up, and demonstrations are given of how they are caught and trained. Then comes the highlight of the event, which is a tug-of-war between 100 men and one elephant. Occasionally it is a fairly even match, but usually the elephant wins hands down!

# 12

# Games and Sports

Thai people are great sports enthusiasts. Nearly all Western games are popular, from soccer to golf. The Thais also enjoy numerous traditional Thai sports, some of which are only played in particular parts of the country.

The best known Thai sport is probably Thai boxing or *Muay Thai*. Every match begins with ritual prayers, followed by homage to the king. Then a small band (usually consisting of a pipe, some drums, and cymbals) strikes up and the fighting begins, to the accompaniment of the music.

Unlike Western boxers, Thai boxers do not just use their fists. Blows with the feet, elbows, and knees are all normal parts of the game. The main skill is in knowing which parts of the body to use for striking the blows. Throwing an opponent, however, usually only results in loss of points.

Thai fencing, *Krabi Krabong*, is probably as old as the Thai nation. A great variety of weapons can be used, such as quarterstaffs, sticks, and wooden spears. But the most usual method of

**Thai boxing. Unlike Western boxers, Thai boxers may use their feet, elbows, and knees in fighting.**

fencing is for each of the fighters to have two wooden sabers, and to hold one in each hand. Like boxing, Thai fencing is always accompanied by music. This begins very slowly, while the fencers make slow, ritual strokes. As the fight becomes more serious, the music is played faster and faster. It reaches an exciting climax when one of the fighters defeats his opponent.

Wickerball or *trakraw* is popular all over the Far East. In fact, it

**The ancient sport of Thai fencing. A variety of weapons may be used and—like Thai boxing—Thai fencing is always accompanied by music.**

forms part of the Asian Games (the Eastern version of the Olympic Games). It is not only played by highly-trained professionals, but is also very popular among ordinary young men, who want to enjoy themselves after work or on the weekends.

There are various forms of *trakraw*, such as net *trakraw* and circle *trakraw*. But the most popular in Thailand is almost certainly loop *trakraw* or *trakraw huang*. A team of seven players stand round a 50-feet (16-meter) diameter circle, and they try to hit a ball through any one of the small hoops which hang 20 feet (six meters) above the ground, without using their hands. However, unlike netball or basketball, the number of points gained varies according to the style and difficulty of the shot. Simply kicking the ball scores lowest, while the highest point scorer is a shot in which the player flings both feet up in a back kick and sends the ball flying up into the ring.

*Sabah* is a game like skittles that is only played during the Songkran festival. Instead of a ball, the flat, hard seed of a huge forest creeper is used. The popularity of the game originally arose from the fact that it was played by both boys and girls. This was considered very daring in the days when girls were normally carefully chaperoned.

The most colorful Thai sport, however, is the traditional kite fighting, *Kaeung-Wau*. This takes place on the Pramane Ground in Bangkok between February and April, when the southeast wind is blowing. Thousands of people come to watch, spreading out their mats on the ground, while hawkers go around trying to sell them cold drinks and prawns.

According to tradition, all Thai kites are either male or female. (This has nothing to do with the bright pictures painted on them, which may be anything from an owl to a cat.) *Chula*, the male kite, can be as long as six and a half feet (two meters) and is shaped like a five-pointed star. *Pakpao*, the female kite, is only about two and a half feet (75 centimeters) long, and roughly the same shape as a conventional kite.

The basic aim of Thai kite flying is to try to drag down the opposing kites. At least two Chula kites have to be flown from one side of a line and four Pakpao kites from the other. The two team captains have to tell the men who actually fly the kites how to maneuver them and the men flying the kites are helped by a number of small boys who run with the string. The Chulas have bamboo barbs attached to the string near the kites. These are designed to entangle and force down the Pakpao kites. But the dainty Pakpaos are very speedy and difficult to catch. They have a semicircular loop with which they can ensnare and drag down the large Chula kites.

The Chulas are usually, but not always, the winners. If two Pakpaos work together they can sometimes snatch an unexpected victory. Whatever the result kite fighting always produces enormous excitement, partly because many of the people watching placed a bet on one of the teams.

There are also several traditional sports involving animals. One

**Bullfighting, Thai style. In Thailand, bullfighting does not mean a bullfighter trying to kill a bull (as it does in Spain). Here, two specially-trained bulls struggle against each other until one of them gives way.**

of them is cockfighting, which is banned in Bangkok but still very popular in the south. It is like cockfighting in Europe in the Middle Ages, and again everyone likes to bet on the result.

Bullfighting, *Chon Wua*, is also popular in the south. Two specially trained bulls lock horns, and each one struggles to make the other give ground. Bullfighting fans will happily spend over eight hours watching fight after fight, and betting on the results. To Western eyes, however, it is a very slow, dull sport.

Fishfighting, *Gad Pla*, is officially banned in most cities, but it still takes place. Two male Siamese fighting fish are put together in a jar, and a life or death battle begins. They are very attractive, large blue and orange freshwater fish. In certain parts of the country they are kept purely as pets, although two males cannot be kept together or they will fight.

# 13

# Entertainment

The artistic life of Thailand came from a mixture of ancient Chinese and Indian influences. In recent years, however, most Thais have been turning more and more to Western forms of entertainment, so the traditional arts are often just tourist attractions.

Classical Thai dancing is an art that has largely died out. But it can still be seen in some places, such as the Lakmuang shrine in Bangkok. Here people pay dancers (who are always on call) to perform traditional steps. This is a way of giving thanks to the spirits for special favors.

The dancing at the Lakmuang shrine is known as *Lakhon* dancing. It is generally performed by an all-female company, wearing glittering costumes and tall pointed headdresses. The story is usually based on a Hindu epic called the *Ramayana*. There is sometimes a little speaking, but usually most of the story is conveyed by movement and gesture.

Another type of classical dancing is the *Khon* or masked dance.

**This picture shows _Lakhon_ dancers wearing glittering costumes and tall pointed headdresses. They act out a story through their movements and gestures.**

This is performed by both men and women, and the principal dancers always wear masks representing either demons or monkeys. Khon dancing is also based on the Ramayana, but it is extremely vigorous and strenuous, and the dancers need years of training before they are ready to perform. The famous fingernail dance originated in the north of Thailand. The dancers (who are all women) wear beautiful golden-colored artificial fingernails, sometimes almost as long as their fingers. Then they make certain stylized movements with their hands as they dance, which not

93

only produce fascinating patterns but also convey traditional ideas.

The traditional music of Thailand has always been played mainly to accompany dancing. Particular types of melodies help to express various moods and actions. For instance, there are seven tunes to show when someone is thinking, 13 to show anger, and no less than 21 to show sorrow or regret. These tunes are played on at least 50 traditional musical instruments. The instruments are all of Indian origin, although only specific instruments are used with any particular dance. For example, the Khon dancing is always accompanied by a piphat orchestra, which consists of one woodwind instrument, some xylophones, and a variety of gongs and drums.

The famous Thai shadow play is called *Nang Talung*, meaning "puppets of animal skin." Life-size puppets made of ox-leather are used, and candles cast their shadows on a screen. Nowadays these shadow plays have almost died out. However, leather puppets of all sizes are still on sale, and are very popular with tourists who like to frame them and hang them on their walls.

Nearly all of Thailand's ancient books were lost when Ayutthaya was sacked in 1767. However, some romantic poetry written in the 17th and 18th centuries still exists as well as a little 18th-century writing. In recent times members of the royal family have been some of the best-known Thai writers. King Rama V (1868 to 1910) was thought to be one of the best authors of his day. His son, Rama VI was also a writer and made some very good translations of Shakespeare.

**Traditional Thai shadow plays have now almost died out, but puppets such as these can still be bought and are popular souvenirs for tourists.**

The first modern novel, *Yellow Race-White Race*, was written by a Thai prince, about his experience as a westernized young Thai man. Since then countless novels, short stories, and biographies have appeared in Thai bookshops, together with many translations of modern Western books.

All the Thai newspaper are published in Bangkok. There are daily papers in the Thai language, Chinese, and English. They are generally written to entertain people rather than to give them information and only about a quarter of a million copies are sold each day.

95

The Thai radio stations are all government controlled. Most of the broadcasts are naturally in Thai, but there are also daily transmissions for several hours in Malay and Chinese. The radio is very popular in Thailand (particularly musical and educational programs), and every village has at least one set which everyone tries to crowd around.

Television began in 1955. Most of the programs shown are made in Thailand, but foreign programs are also shown, including American cartoons, which are extremely popular with the Thai children.

# 14

# The Land of Smiles

Here is a list of dos and don'ts for visitors to Thailand. Most of them probably seem trivial, but they are all extremely important to the Thais.

First and foremost, the monarchy is greatly revered. So the slightest disrespect, even to a coin bearing the king's head, could have serious consequences.

Similarly, religion plays a very important part in Thai life. This means that visitors must be careful not to offend against any religious custom or practice. For example, visitors must never go into a temple wearing shorts or low-cut dresses, but must dress discreetly and modestly, however hot and sticky the weather. Also visitors must take off their shoes before entering the inner part of the temple. And women must remember not to speak directly to a monk or a novice, and certainly must not touch him. In fact, if a woman wants to give anything to a monk she must ask a man to tell him to spread out part of his saffron robe and then she can place her gift on that.

To Thais the head is the most important part of the body. So no one must ever touch another person, even a child, on the head. Thai people themselves always try to keep their heads lower than the head of any person who is older or more important than they are, to show their respect for him. In the same way there are rules concerning the feet. These are considered lowly, and must never be used, for example, for holding back a door. Moreover, no one must ever sit with their feet pointing toward a statue in a temple, or at some other person, but must always tuck them underneath their body.

When Thais meet each other, they do not shake hands or embrace as people in the West would. Demonstrations of affection are not allowed in public in Thailand. Only very Westernized young Thais would even dare to hold hands in the street, and touching other people at all is unusual. The most usual form of greeting is the *wai* greeting. In this, each person puts their hands together—as if saying a prayer—and bows to the other person. In recent years, however, some Thais have begun shaking hands with foreigners, instead of giving the traditional *wai* greeting, to make the visitors feel at home.

How much longer will these rules last? Nobody knows. Most of them are very old and it seems as if they will go on for ever. But the number of tourists in Thailand has doubled in less than twenty years, and while the tourists are learning about Thailand, the Thais are also learning about the ways of the rest of the world.

# GLOSSARY

| | |
|---:|:---|
| *chedi* | Pagoda |
| **joss stick** | Slender stick of incense |
| **klongs** | Canals |
| **latex** | The liquid from the rubber plant used to produce rubber |
| **Nirvana** | State of perfect knowledge and happiness in Buddhism |
| *prik-kee-nooh* | Tiny red or green chili pepper that Thais add to most of their food |
| *samlor* | A small three-wheeled vehicle which the driver pedals like a bicycle |
| *sampans* | Long, narrow boats |
| **spill** | Slender piece of wood |
| *wat* | Buddhist temple |

# INDEX